MW01171145

The Ugliest Man God Made

Principles to Help Resolve Identity Issues

By Donald A. Peart

The Ugliest Man God Ever Made — A Principle to Help Resolve Identity Issues© 2016 Donald A. Peart

ISBN: 9781091587748

Acknowledgment

"For it seemed good to the Holy Spirit..." (Acts 15:28a). It is the Spirit of Jesus who revealed the contents of the book; and caused His Word to heal me of my inner and outwards struggles!

Honors

It is with great gratitude that I say Jesus Christ, the Son of the living God, is the highest value in my life. I (We) love Him because he loved us first! It is He, the living Christ, that has made me a better person towards Him, towards our fellow humanity and towards all His creation. The Spirit of Jesus is my foremost Teacher!

I honor Judy, my beautiful wife of 36 years, and my best friend. I also honor our six children (Donald Jr. and his wife Keyanna, Jeshua, Charity, Benjamin, and Jesse) who have experienced the demands of ministry with us. I also mention our current grandchildren: Skye Marie Peart, Justus John Peart, and Selah Peart. I honor my parents Lennox Peart and Millicent Peart who the Lord selected to use as portals to send me into the earth in order for me to complete the will of the Lord Jesus.

I also honor the men and women of God who have imparted to me through the years — Steve Daniel, Raymond Buie, Kelley Varner, Turnel Nelson, Sandra Hayden, Earl Palmer, Clarice Fluitt, Myles Monroe, Steve Everette, Don Nori, Dave Dayton, Raj Ramlal, Vishnu Seepersad and Samuel Soleyn. Special thanks to Ramcharitair Merhair for helping with the edit of this book.

Contents

Introduction

*Ecclesiastes3:11: [God] has made **everything beautiful** in his time....*

"Ugliness" versus "beauty," according to the definition of a respective society is relative. Beauty to one person may be ugliness to another. Ugliness to one person may be beauty to another. Thus, the phrase "beauty is in the eye of the beholder" is true.

With respect to human beauty or human ugliness (as defined by society), my wife, Judith, has a saying, "there is someone for each person." In other words, what one person may deem as too ugly to date (as an example); to another, that person may be acceptable.

The heavenly Father, God, made it clear in the Scriptures that "he has made everything beautiful in His time." That is, there is God's set time ("His time") for each person to be introduced into the earth, through birth; and in His mind, our time is "beautiful."

God sees every human as beautiful. They are all made in His image and likeness. Yet, we see so many issues relating to beauty and ugliness that may result in rejection and self-esteem issues.

1

One of the direct results of sin was self-rejection and feeling shameful of one's apparent nakedness (ugliness). Before Mr. and Mrs. Adam sinned, they were God conscious; and they were "both naked and not ashamed." After they sinned, they became self-conscious and fearful. So much so, that they hid from God, and covered themselves with fig leaves.

*Genesis 2:24: And they were both naked, the man and his wife, and were **not ashamed.***

It is clear from the verse above that Mr. and Mrs. Adam were not ashamed of any party of their body. They were not even ashamed to go about naked. They were secured in their appearance in God's love! However, after they ate from the tree that was placed off limit, they were "told" the ability to see both good and bad; rather than seeing themselves as the image and likeness of God.

*Genesis 3:7: And the eyes of them both were opened, and **they knew that they were naked;** and they sewed fig leaves together and **made themselves aprons** ....*

How many today are covering or hiding themselves? Today it is rare to find a person who is not covering up something about themselves, all in the name of being "accepted." Some marry the wrong person. That is, in the dating process, in order to prevent rejection, some may cover their true nature (their nakedness); however, after marriage, the true self comes out that may cause conflicts within the marriage.

Genesis 3:10-11: [10]*And [Adam] said, I heard thy voice in the garden, and I was **afraid**, because I was naked; **and I hid myself.** [11]And he said, who told you that you were naked?*

Adam "hid himself;" that is. Adam rejected himself; and he left God's unconditional love which would have "cast out"[1] all of his "fear." It is also apparent that there was something or someone "who told" Adam that he was naked. That is, is there an inner voice in you telling you are ugly? God's ultimate remedy for humanity rejecting themselves is Jesus Christ taking on our sin that causes ugliness.

The fact that Jesus experienced our ugliness, as a man, He is now able to comfort and heal any who may feel that they are too ugly relative to the world's standard, an ugliness that may cause some to commit or consider suicide. This ugliness may range from an apparently ugly face, ugly

---

[1] 1 John 4:18

nose, ugly feet, ugly financial situation, ugly poverty, ugly skin colors, ugly rape, ugly abortion(s), ugly prejudices, and so on, and so on. Hence, the Scriptures teaches that Jesus is the ugliest man God made! Why? So, Jesus can identify with all ugliness and heal any ugliness in those who would come to Him for His aid.

Thus, as you read this book, some statements may shock you; you may cry, you may experience again your past pains, and so forth; however, please be patient and finish this synoptic book on our Lord Jesus' ugliness. Jesus did not come as a beautiful prince. Instead, the heavenly Father sent the Lord Jesus in things related to ugliness.

The Ugliest Man

*Isaiah 52:14, NKJV: **Just as** many were astonished at you, **so His visage was marred more than any man,** And His form more than the sons of men.*

*Isaiah 52:14, LXX: As many shall be amazed at you, **so shall your face be without glory from men**, and your glory [shall not be honored] by the sons of men.*

*Isaiah 52:14, LXX[2]: In which manner shall be amazed by you many, **so shall be despised by men the sight of your appearance,** and your glory by the sons of men.*

Jesus Christ (the Lamb of God) is the ugliest man God made. This is revealed in the Hebrew text of Isaiah 52:14. Yes! There is none born as ugly as He, neither will there be any created as ugly. This apparent ugliness ranges from an ugly appearance to ugly circumstances in Jesus' life.

For example, the Holy Spirit conceived Him while Mary was betrothed. He slept on rocks. He had no certain dwelling place, and so on. I know, for some, this is hard to believe. Some may also say, "I thought Jesus has blond hair and blue

---

[2]http://www.bayithamashiyach.com/index.html

5

eyes." Or some may say, "Jesus is black, with Jamaican dreadlocks." **The answer to both of these statements is no!** Jesus, the Christ, does not have blond hair or blue eyes; neither is he black with Jamaican dreadlocks. Jesus is the ugliest man God ever made. Jesus came through the lineage of the Jews that was mixed[3] with Syrians, Hittites, Canaanites, Moabites, and so on. With that said, I have made some bold statements with respect to the Scripture cited above (Isaiah 52:14), indicating that "Jesus was the ugliest man God ever made." So, as we proceed to understand my statement, allow me to clarify Isaiah 52:14.

Isaiah 54:14 can be a little confusing as to who is the "you" in Isaiah 52:14. The verse reads: "just as many were astonished at you." This apparent confusion of who is the subject of Isaiah 52:14 through Isaiah 53 was also experienced by another person; and this "confusion" was documented as such. Thus, I want to take the time to clarify who the "you" is in the first part of the verse and who is the "Him" or who is the "your" is in the phrase "your face" in the Septuagint translation. Here is the question, was

---

[3]This apparent "ugly lineage" (mixed) will also be discussed later to refute those who are bigots concerning race

this verse referring to Isaiah or Jesus? **The answer is yes!** The Ethiopian eunuch who Philip led to the Lord in Acts 8:27-39 had a similar question, as he read Isaiah 52 and Isaiah 53.

*Acts 8:34, KJV: And the eunuch answered Philip, and said, I pray thee, of whom speaks the prophet this; **of himself, or of some other man?***

The fact that the eunuch could not clarify if the Scriptures he was reading was referring to Isaiah or Jesus is borne out in the Scripture reference. You see, the Scripture depiction (Isaiah 52:14) used Isaiah's personal appearance as a pre-figure of what the Messiah—Jesus—would look like. Thus, in the first part of Isaiah 52:14, the "you" is Isaiah; and as the Scripture continues, the focus was turned to **Jesus** ("Him" or "your face," or "your appearance," as it should.

*Acts 8:35, KJV: Then Philip opened his mouth, and began at the same Scripture, and preached unto him **Jesus.***

Philip went straight to the most important person in the Scripture reference—Jesus; probably because of the eunuch's travel plan heading to Ethiopia. Hence, the Holy Spirit directed Philip to leave the citywide revival to catch up and witness to this one important "Black" man.

7

Yet, Isaiah was an integral part of the narrative. Isaiah wrote the verses in discussion through the Holy Spirit; and Isaiah was an example of the Messiah's ugliness. People apparently were stunned at Isaiah's appearance, so much so that the Lord mentioned that fact in the Scripture

"Just as many were astonished at you (Isaiah), so His (Jesus') visage was marred more than any man, And His (Jesus') form more than the sons of men."

As Isaiah was not a pretty sight to behold, so Jesus was not a pretty sight to behold, in the natural world. Or should, I say, Jesus' ugliness and disfigured appearance was also seen in Isaiah. God asked Isaiah to walk around naked for three (3) years; and apparently, Isaiah was not a pretty sight to look at. In fact, Isaiah's neighbors ("many" of them) were astonished at his ugly nakedness. Thus, the Lord used Isaiah's ugly nakedness as an example of the ugliness Jesus, would also experience.

Isaiah 20:1-4, NAS: ¹In the year that the commander came to Ashdod, when Sargon the king of Assyria sent him and he fought against Ashdod and captured it, ²at that time the LORD spoke through Isaiah the son of Amoz, saying, "Go and loosen the sackcloth from your hips and take your shoes off your feet." And he did so, going naked and barefoot. ³And the LORD said,

"Even as My servant Isaiah has gone naked and barefoot three years as a sign and token against Egypt and Cush, [4]so the king of Assyria will lead away the captives of Egypt and the exiles of Cush, young and old, naked and barefoot with buttocks uncovered, to the shame of Egypt.

Disfigured Appearance

Isaiah 52:14, NKJV: **Just as** *many were astonished at* **you, so His visage was marred more than any man,** *And His form more than the sons of men.*

The Lord says, "Just as many were astonished at **you,** so His visage was marred more than any man." **"You"** who? "You" Isaiah! The verse is saying, Isaiah, just **as** many were stunned at you, "So **His visage (lit., beauty)** was **marred more** than any man." As seen in the preceding chapter, the **"His"** in this part of the verse refers to **Jesus, the Lamb of God.**

Traditionally, the elders taught that the **marring** took place during the time of Jesus' capture up to His crucifixion. This is true, but not complete. To completely understand the truth of this Scripture, it must be fully interpreted.

The verse above can be interpreted as follows: Just as many were stunned at Isaiah's visage (beauty, appearance), so will "many" be stunned at "His" (Jesus') appearance. Again, as briefly discussed in the previous chapter, according to the Scripture, Isaiah was an ugly man. Isaiah was so ugly that people were stunned at his appearance. And, by the way, the people of his day saw Isaiah's apparent ugly body; and so, from reading the Scripture reference of Isaiah 52:14, it can be determined that Isaiah's body was not a pretty sight.

Isaiah 20:2-3, NKJV: *²At the same time the LORD spoke by Isaiah the son of Amoz, saying, "Go, and remove the sackcloth from your body, and take your sandals off your feet."* ***And he did so, walking naked and barefoot.*** *³Then the LORD said, "****Just as*** *My servant Isaiah has walked naked and barefoot **three years** for a sign and a wonder against Egypt and Ethiopia; so, shall the king of Assyria lead away the Egyptian prisoners."*

The Lord used the same phrase **"just as"** in Isaiah 20:3 that he also used in Isaiah 52:14 when He indicated to Isaiah that Isaiah's ugliness was foreshadowing Christ's ugliness. Remember, the Lord said to Isaiah, **"Just as** many were astonished at **you...."** **So, the question must be asked,** when were they astonished at Isaiah? The answer is: **"Just as"** the three years Isaiah "walked naked and barefoot"

Yes! For three years he walked naked; and they saw his deformed body. Therefore, not only did Isaiah's words point to the Messiah, but his very bodily shape was also representative, to a degree, of Jesus' ugliness. Isaiah was not a pretty sight to look at.

11

In like manner, the people were also stunned at Jesus' ugliness. This happened before His "Passion," as you can see. Why were they stunned at the Lord's appearance? The answer is the Lord's appearance "was marred (lit., disfigured) more than **any** man." Jesus' **visage (lit., face, beauty, appearance)** was disfigured more than any man. Do you see it? Listen to the rest of the verse, "and his form (lit., outline, delineation) **more than** the sons of men."

The Lamb's outline (bodily shape) was **"more"** deformed than any son or daughter of men to ever be born on this earth. As stated above, His outline (His bodily appearance) is disfigured **"more than"** any man who will ever exist.

This may include His face, His build, His arms, His legs, and every other physical part of Him. The Scripture teaches that there is a reason for this truth, as you will see later. That is, we will see that Jesus can identify and give identity to those who struggle with self-esteem issues. However, let us first look at this truth of Jesus' ugliness from some other verses.

Ugly Root, Dry Ground

*Isaiah 53:2, NKJV: For He shall grow up before Him as a tender plant, and as a root out of dry ground. He has no **form** or **comeliness**; and when we see Him, there is no beauty that we should desire Him.*

*Isaiah 53:2, LXX: We announced as of a male child before him, as a root in a land thirsting. **There is no appearance to him, nor glory;** and we beheld him, and he does not have appearance nor beauty.*

We see here the Lord is symbolically called a "root" that came out of "dry ground." This is significant, especially if one looks at it allegorically. First, one must note as stated above, the word "root" is **representative** (symbolic, simile, allegorical, parable) of the Man, Jesus.

Therefore, the words "dry ground" can also be a representation or symbol if interpretation of the verse is to be consistent. To see this point of view (understanding) clearly, let us look in the book of beginnings (Genesis) for an interpretation.

*Genesis 2:6-7, NKJV: ⁶**But** a mist went up from the earth and watered **(lit., to quaff — to drink deeply to guzzle)** the whole face of the ground. ⁷**And** the LORD God formed man of the **dust (or mud)** of the ground and breathed into his nostrils the breath of life; and man became a living being.*

First, **the word "But"** in verse six is the same Hebrew prefix translated **"And"** in verse seven. Therefore, verse six is not a contrast to verse seven, however, a continuation. Also, you can logically see that the action of verse seven took place after the action of verse six. Now, let us look at these verses in more detail.

The Lord caused the earth to be **"watered"** or "to drink water deeply."   So, Adam came out of **"deep"** dirt (compare Psalm 42:7). Thus, the water that was produced from the mist apparently also had the ability to moisten deep" into the earth. The Father wanted the dry earth to become wet ground (mud). In the words of the King James Version, the earth was "watered." Therefore, it was from the "watered" (or moist) ground that the Lord **formed** Adam. Do you see it?

Let's look at the order again:

1. The water from the mist (cloud or fog) watered the earth.
2. **Afterwards,** "the Lord God formed (lit., to mold, or shape by squeezing) man of the **dust** (lit., mud) of the ground."

The word **"dust"** in verse seven is also defined as **"mud,"** according to Strong's Concordance, #6083. This is a solid definition because of what

14

happened in Genesis 2:6.   That is, water mixed with dirt equals mud. This enabled God to shape, mold and **beautify Adam** into the predetermined figure He wanted. Any vessel on a potter's wheel can easily be worked into any shape if the clay is moist. God was that Potter with Adam; as he was the Potter with Jesus.

However, Jesus was molded in the hand of "the Potter" from "dry ground." Now, we know from a practical point of view that a person cannot mold dry ground. However, God is not a man; and as it is written, "all things are possible with God." Thus, the "molding" of Jesus from dry ground is seen allegorically of the root (Jesus) that grew up out of the dry ground.

A root, in a dry (parched) ground, is usually discolored and ugly. The dry ground can point to the fact that **Jesus was not formed beautifully,** as was the first Adam.

In other words, it is difficult, if not impossible with man, not God, to mold or shape dry dirt. God formed Jesus out of dry ground. Therefore, our Lord had "no form or comeliness" (Isaiah 53:2, NKJV). He had "no form" because, it is difficult to mold dry ground into a particular form; I say this speaking allegorically. On the other hand, wet dirt, or clay in the hand of a potter can easily be beautified. Do you see it? If that is understood, let us look at the important Septuagint translation, the translation that Jesus and His early apostles used.

*Isaiah 53:2, NKJV: For He shall grow up before Him as a tender plant, and as a root out of dry ground. He has no **form** or **comeliness** ....*

*Isaiah 53:2, LXX: We announced as of a male child before him, as a root in a land thirsting. **There is no appearance to him, nor glory** ....*

In addition, the LXX translated the phrase "For He shall grow up before Him as **a tender plant,** and as a root out of dry ground" to "We announced as of **a male child** before him, as a root in a land thirsting." "The tender plant" is equivalent to the "male child" Jesus. This male child (Jesus) had "no appearance to Him, nor glory" (he was a root out of dry ground) as a child; yet he was still considered "tender" as a male child. Think of the conflict in Mary and Joseph.

Jesus was apparently a dry root (not appealing in appearance)' Yet, Mary and Joseph saw Jesus as a tender plant. In other words, think of the apparent love and obedience that Mary and Joseph had towards God, even after they saw what the male child, Jesus, looked like at birth.

16

Jesus was apparently not pretty at birth. Jesus may have been looked at as a "felled" tree. How did I come to this by the Spirit of Jesus? The Hebrew word "tender" translated as "male child" literally means to suck milk, or to give milk. According to Strong's dictionary, the word carries the idea of a "felled tree" that a twig grows out of.

A picture or understanding being conveyed is that of a person laying on his/her side like a "felled tree "receiving milk from a mother. Thus, in the state of being a male child, Jesus had no form or beauty, and therefore, rejected by some; however, he was comforted through Mary, with the unconditional love of a mother

There was "no appearance to Him, nor glory;" yet, it can also be argued that due to Jesus' ugliness at birth, the Father gave Him hope upon Mary's breast, according to the Messianic Psalm.

Psalms 22:9-10, KJV: [9]But you he that took me out of the womb; you did make me **hope upon my mother's breasts.** *[10]I* **was cast upon you from the womb***; you my God from my mother's belly.*

Why was Jesus cast upon God from the womb" Why was God, His God from His mother's belly? God was Jesus' Father, yes! Yet in light of Isaiah 53:2, more can be understood about the apparent rejection of Jesus, maybe, because of His looks. That is, Jesus "was cast upon [God] from the womb;" yet the Father did not leave Jesus comfortless. God made Him "**hope upon His mother's breasts.**"

A point in understanding this truth is that Jesus can comfort even children who were discarded by their parents and/or families for whatever reason. Jesus can comfort children who are treated badly; because they may not look like the accepted beauty standard.

According to Hebrews 4:15, "He can be touched with the feelings of our 'weaknesses'." He was "in all points tempted as we." The Father allowed the Lamb of God (Jesus) to experience every test and temptation of ugliness that humanity would experience with a view to heal as many as He can from low self-esteem.

So Ugly, No Representative

*Isaiah 53:2, NKJV: For He shall grow up before Him as a tender plant, And as a root out of dry ground. He has no **form (lit., representation)** or comeliness; and when we see Him, there is no beauty that we should desire Him.*

Jesus had no exact **representation** of Himself; even though Isaiah's appearance was used as a "type of Jesus; yet Isaiah's similarity was nothing like what our Messiah suffered for us. Yes, there is **"no representation"** for Jesus; yet men like to draw handsome pictures of Jesus. In Ezekiel's day, Israel also worshiped pictures of handsome men portrayed on walls.

These were images of the Chaldean (Babylonian) men, with the understanding that the "Chaldean men" represents apostate men in "Mystery Babylon," described in the book of Revelation. The Israelites loved to worship the beauty of men (Isaiah 44:13), rather than the living God. So, likewise, in our day, people gloat over outward beauty; and put down those some of are not of the standard of the day. Per the Scriptures, this kind of attitude (worshiping images of beauty) creates whoredom in people.

19

*Isaiah 44:13, KJV: The carpenter stretches out [his] rule; he marks it out with a line; he fits it with planes, and he marks it out with the 'circle-former,' and makes it after **the figure of a man,** according to the **beauty of a man** that it may remain in the house.*

*Ezekiel 23:14-15, NKJV: [14]But she increased her harlotry; she looked at **men portrayed on the wall,** Images of Chaldeans portrayed in vermilion, [15]Girded with belts around their waists, Flowing turbans on their heads, all of them **looking like captains,** in the manner of the **Babylonians** of Chaldea, the land of their nativity.*

The children of Israel worshiped idols that looked like handsome men, and they worshiped the pictures of men upon the walls of Babylon. These idols and images were handsome figures "looking like captains (lit.; generals);" meaning they were handsome pictures to look at, like a man in military outfit.

So likewise, **Mystery Babylon** (a symbol of the many apostate religions and denominations that exists today has made their beautified images of their idols; and/or beautiful and false images of **"their"** Jesus—which is "another Jesus" (Revelation17:1-5).With respect to "another Jesus," Mystery Babylon does claim to have "the light of a lamp" and the "voice of the bridegroom"—Jesus (compare Revelation 18:23

w/Matthew 9:14-15). However, this "voice" and "light" is not the true representation of Jesus. According to Paul, we must not be ignorant of the fact that some do preach "another Jesus" and "a different gospel."

*2 Corinthians 11:3-4, KJV: ³But I fear, lest by any means, as the **serpent** beguiled Eve through his subtlety, so your minds should be corrupted from the simplicity that is in Christ ⁴For if he that cometh preaches **another Jesus,** whom we have not preached, or [if] you **receive another spirit,** which you have not received, or another gospel, which you have not accepted, you might well bear with [him].*

Man has also developed "another Jesus" that denies the ugliness of suffering **for** our Lord. They have also developed a "different gospel" that denies Jesus' ugliness by preaching the beauty of wealth as the measure of godliness. Some have gone as far as making idols of baby Jesus that many worship. Jesus is no longer a baby.

We are to emphasize his death, burial, and resurrection. It is written: *"The day of death better than the day of birth" (Ecclesiastes 7:1b, NIV).* Some have also made statues of Mary, pictures of Jesus to hang on the wall, and so on. These modern images of "**their**" unbiblical Jesus are "portrayed on the wall" — the wall(s) of Churches, and homes, giving a false representation of Jesus.

Some in the Church are worshiping these beautiful Babylonian images. As Ezekiel said, "She (some in the Church) increased her harlotry," by committing whoredom with manmade images. Images of the Black Jesus and the White Jesus are wrong! An idol of the so-called, baby Jesus that some worship is wrong! These images are made after "corruptible man" by corrupt man (Romans 1:23). In fact, the Lord commands us not to corrupt His image by making images (i.e., pictures and statues).

Deuteronomy 4:15-16, KJV: [15]*Take you therefore good heed unto yourself, for you saw no manner of similitude on the day that the Lord spoke unto you in Horeb out of the midst of fire.* [16]**Lest you corrupt yourselves,** *and make you a graven image, the similitude of any figure, the likeness of male and female.*

Deuteronomy 4:15-16, NKJV: [15]*Take careful heed to yourselves, for* **you saw no form**[4] **when the LORD** *spoke to you at Horeb out of the midst of the fire,* [16]**lest**

[4]"Form" is defined from a Hebrew root word that means to "species" (Strong's #8544, #4327). From God came all species, and all humanity is from "one blood" (Acts 17:26)

22

you act corruptly and *make for yourselves a carved image in the form of any figure: the likeness of male or female.*

We are warned not to pursue to **know** Jesus according to His fleshly appearance. "'So-that from now,' **know we no man after the flesh;** yes, though we have known Christ after the flesh, yet now, we-know [Him] no more" (2 Corinthians 5:17).

God Himself warned mankind not to make any images of Him. He called it a corrupt act to do so. His words are: "Lest you act corruptly." The question is, lest you act corruptly in what? "Lest you act" **corrupt** by making false images or false similitude of God according to the standards of corrupt mankind (Romans 1:23).

Remember, the children of Israel did not see any bodily representation of God in Mount Horeb. God did not want them to corrupt the image of Him. There is only one true image of God, Jesus — the Lamb of God (Colossians 1:15; Hebrews 1:2-4). Other images of Jesus made by man are always corruptible.

*Romans 1:23, NKJV: And **changed** the glory of the incorruptible God into an **image** made like **corruptible man** — and birds and four-footed animals and creeping things.*

Any image of Jesus, made by man, is corruptible. The Black Jesus and the White Jesus, these images are corruptible. Why? "He (Jesus) has no form (lit., representation)." The word **"form"** also means "delineation" according to Strong's dictionary.

"Delineation" means the act of representing. None have represented the maimed Lamb bodily; neither will any represent Him. To God, man's image of Jesus is corruptible (Romans 1:23). **This generation did not see Jesus; therefore, we do not have the right to make any corrupt icons.**

Deuteronomy teaches that humanity will corrupt God's image, and themselves, especially, when they make Him to look like any similitude of "male" and "female." Two reasons for this that I have found are:

1. Only God knew how Jesus would look when He came to the earth

2. After Adam sinned, he birthed children "in his **own likeness**[5] and after **his image**,"[6] not God's image (Genesis 5:3).

The image of man (Adam's) is opposite the image of God (Christ). One must remember God appears irregular compared to man. For example, God's day **begins** in the **evening** and **ends** in the **morning** (Genesis 1). A good way of looking at this truth is that when some want to sleep, God wants to talk. God is opposite to sinful man.

God's truth concerning Jesus is also the opposite men's doctrines being taught today. The doctrines of some men teach that Jesus is handsome relative to their standard, but God is opposite this. The proof is He made our Lord the most disfigured man who ever lived or will live (Isaiah 52:14).

There is no form (representation or outline) for Jesus. God made Him disfigured; thus, it is difficult to copy His image. It was also difficult for people to look at His face. Jesus was so ugly man despised Him and hid their faces from Him.

---

[5] The Hebrew word for "likeness" relates to blood
[6] The Hebrew word for "image" relates to "phantom" (spirit)

It took someone hungry for God's true beauty to look past Jesus' physical ugliness.

> "And this is the will of him that sent me, that everyone who **sees** the Son, and believes **into** him, may have everlasting life: and I will raise him up at the last day" (John 6:40).

In light of the subject of this book; and referencing the Scripture above, coupled with Isaiah 52:14 and Isaiah 53:1-2, Jesus' appearance was such that a person had to consider what he/she was seeing of Jesus; and then couple that "sight" with faith in Jesus.

This shows the truth that one must be able to "see" inner beauty in all of God's creation, regardless of the external appearance. Even though Jesus was disfigured bodily, the beauty of **God's express image (lit., character; Hebrews 1:3),** radiated from Him. The inward character of the Lamb of God was so beautiful, people flocked to Him. All who believed in the Lord, when He walked the earth as a man, had to look past His disfigurement. However, there were many who were stunned at his "marred" (disfigured) "visage" (or beauty). Yet, the beauty of this was that, through this ugliness, the Lamb of God was able to sprinkle many.

*Hebrews 10:22, KJV: Let us draw near with a true heart in full assurance of faith, having our hearts **sprinkled** from an evil conscience, and our bodies washed with pure water.*

*Isaiah 52:14-15, KJV: [14]As many were 'stunned' at you; his 'beauty' was so marred more than any man, and his form more than the sons of men; [15]**So shall he sprinkle many nations** ....*

The Scripture first describes Jesus' ugliness. Then it says, **"So shall he sprinkle many nations."** One might ask, "How does the Lamb's ugliness sprinkle many nations?" **An** interpretation is this: Because of His ugliness, He is able to **"sprinkle,"** that is, heal with His **blood.** He is able to heal those who feel they are ugly, both physically and ugly circumstances. Thus, comfort comes to those who allow Him to heal them by his blood.

Another way Jesus heals those with self-esteem problems is: He can inform the believer as to why He created body parts. For example, the Lord made the **nose to breathe** (in God's breath Genesis 2:7). He made the **eyes to see** (God) Matthew 5:8, Revelation 1:12). **The hair is for covering,** or protection (2 Kings 1:8, Matthew 3:4). Finally, the **mouth was created to speak** (praises to God, etc., Psalm 149:6), and **the ear to hear** (Revelation 2:29).

Therefore, do not despise your looks, or anyone else's. One should not even feel deprived relative to someone else. If one despises his, or her looks, they are actually despising the image of God (Genesis 1:27). If anyone feels he/she is not beautiful according to today's standard, remember God makes nothing ugly. "He hath made **everything beautiful** in his time" (Ecclesiastes 3:11). Yet, if one is handsome or beautiful, he/she should walk in that beauty. Esther, Daniel, Mishael, Hananiah and Azariah were good looking (Esther 2:7, Daniel 1:4). David was handsome (I Samuel 16:12), and God used David and the others, mightily.

Joseph and his mother were good-looking (Genesis 39:6; 29:17), yet God guided him to rulership. But note, even though David and Joseph were handsome, it was their heart (inward beauty) that attracted God to them (I Samuel 16: 7-12, Genesis 39:1-13).

The point is this: whether one is ugly or good-looking according to today's standards, "He (God) hath **made everything beautiful in his time..." (Ecclesiastes 3:11).** To God, everyone who is born on earth is beautiful.

All are created in His image and likeness,[7] and God is not ugly according to man's standards. We are **"fearfully and wonderfully made"** by God (Psalm 139:14). In other words, when God made you, He was too **fearful** to make a mistake. Thus, however you may look; it is **"wonderfully"** beautiful to God. He sees Himself in you!

---

[7] Note: I previously stated that Genesis 5:3 indicates Mr. and Mrs. Adam reproduced children after their image and likeness, yet according to James 3:9, mankind still has the similitude of God in them. Hence, the dual nature (dual image) in humanity has to be morphed into the image of God's Son, Jesus (Romans 8:29).

Too Ugly to Look at!

Isaiah 53:3, NKJV: He is despised and rejected by men, a Man of sorrows and acquainted with grief. **And we hid, as it were, our faces from Him;** *He was despised, and we did not esteem Him.*

One can see from this verse, that our Lord Jesus was rejected and despised. Those who saw Him hid their faces from Him. It is apparent that one of the reasons why men hid their faces from Him was Jesus' ugliness. We learned this earlier from Isaiah 52:14, and Isaiah 53:2.

Jesus was so ugly bodily that sometimes men could not bear to look at Him. Listen to an interpretation: "And we hid, as it were, our faces from Him (because of his ugliness); He was despised (because of His ugliness), and we did not esteem Him (because of His ugliness)." Man! Can one imagine the pain Jesus felt when men rejected Him! Can we imagine the pain some feel today because they are deemed ugly and may be rejected because of their ugly circumstances! So why did they reject Jesus? **He was too ugly to look at!** Let me tell you about an event.

This event happened to me, at a time in my life when I was struggling with my own self-esteem. After I got out of the United States Marine Corps,

I experienced poverty that eventually caused me to hate myself. However, God used this impoverished situation to help heal my mind. In my mind, I was treating people the way I felt about myself. I realized that the bad feeling I had towards myself, is the way I may have been previously treating the poor. Therefore, God used the situation to heal me. Thus, I can now help someone else. With that said, the event took place my first year in Engineering School.

One day, while waiting for a Math class to begin, a young man (an angel, Hebrews 13:1) came to me asking for directions. The man was so disfigured in the face that it was difficult for me to look at him. I was so "stunned" (compare Isaiah 52:14) at his disfigurement, to the point that I did't even want to talk to him or be seen with him.

Because of these inner feelings, I began to cry within, holding back the tears without. These emotions I was feeling while talking with the young man was related to an understanding of the Lord's ugliness that was unveiled to me the night before.

I felt, in my heart, that I had denied the Lord. Again, the reason this denial was so disturbing to me was the Lord had taught me about Jesus' ugliness the night before I met this young man.

The Lord instructed me the night before of His ugliness to comfort me in my ugliness (my ugly situation that eventually affected my self-esteem). Thus, in my rejection of the young man, I fulfilled the Scripture in Isaiah 53:3; in essence, I rejected Jesus' ugliness also. "And **we** hid as it were our faces from Him...." Yes, all of **"we"** (us) have denied the Lord's ugliness.

Yes! All of "we" are sometimes still ashamed of Him. If anyone does not believe that we **all** denied Him (His ugliness), take a look at the pictures of Jesus those men and women have on their walls. Some have Him portrayed as a handsome Black man, or a good-looking white man. These pictures deny the true look of Jesus' ugliness.

Nonetheless, I did embrace the young man's disfigurement, and I helped him; after I heard those words resound in me ("And **we** hid as it were our faces from Him"); and these words I heard internally also corrected me.

I did eventually get myself together and helped the young man find the room he was looking for. In helping him, I embraced myself. But the idea that I had denied the Lord's ugliness was painful. My mind flashed back to the Scriptures (I was searching for how Jesus must have felt). I realized

He was "a man of sorrows" (Isaiah 53:3; 2 Corinthians 6:10). The young man was an angel sent by God. He entered the rooms he asked me to help him find; and he did not exit the room; and I never saw him again on campus or off campus. He was apparently a **stranger** the Lord deliberately sent to test me; and to heal me.

*Hebrews 13:2, KJV: Be not forgetful to entertain strangers; for thereby some have entertained **angels** unawares.*

Again, it is my understanding that this angel was sent to test and heal my acceptance of Jesus' ugliness. Thus, once I embraced the Messiah's ugliness, I was able to embrace myself and my impoverished circumstances at that time. The Scripture says, He carried our sorrows. Therefore, He could identify with my feelings and give me peace. Jesus healed me!

His Ugliness, Our Peace

*Isaiah 53:4, NKJV: ⁴Surely He has borne our griefs and carried our sorrows; **yet we esteemed Him** stricken, smitten by God, and afflicted. ⁵But He was wounded for our transgressions, He was bruised for our iniquities; **the chastisement for our peace was upon Him,** and by His stripes we are healed.*

The verses above are highlights of Jesus' sufferings while upon the earth, including, but not limited to, the cross. Yet, if one will note, He was ordained to suffer before the foundation of the world (1 Peter 1:20). The Book of Revelation, Chapter 13 says, He was a "Lamb slain (or maimed) **from the foundation** of the world."

Therefore, one can see truth in Isaiah 53:4, concerning things that happened in the **invisible, which** were manifested in the visible, almost two thousand years ago.

My point is this: Jesus was also manifested in the earth with "the chastisement for our peace upon Him."   In the text above, Jesus carried our grief and sorrows. According to the subject of this book, the sorrows He carried include, but not limited to, the sorrow of ugliness; or the sorrow of self-esteem problems.

That is, He was able to hear and carry the way people felt about His disfigurement. His ugliness was so mind boggling, people thought Him to be plagued, smitten, and cursed by God (see Isaiah 53:4 above). "But he was wounded for our transgression, he was bruised for our iniquities: the chastisement of our peace was upon him; and with his stripes we are healed" (Rev. 13:8; Isaiah 53:5).

We can have peace in our ugliness; because the chastisement of our peace was upon Him, bodily. He can heal anyone who feels ugly or has low self-esteem. Remember, Jesus, Himself was **not esteemed** by men (Isaiah 53:4). **He was smitten (i.e. made ugly by God, for our healing).** It is written, "And by His stripes we are healed" (Isaiah 53:4). The Scripture also says, **"Surely He** has borne our griefs, and **carried our sorrows...."**

Yes, this speaks of the sorrow of ugliness, which plagues mankind, and the sorrow of self-esteem problems that cause some people to become promiscuous just to be accepted. Jesus can heal you and give you peace about your self-worth. He felt every sorrow anyone would ever feel.

Therefore, he can **"sympathize"** with our weakness (Hebrews 4:15, NKJV, NIV). He can be **"touched"** (KJV) with what you feel. He can sympathize with our emotional challenges. There is a real and living flesh and **bone** Jesus in heaven, who is empathic towards us (Luke 24:39-41). He is not a spirit who has not felt your pain. So, reach out and **"touch Him"** (compare John 20:25-27).

He Embraces our Ugliness

*Hebrews 4:15, KJV: For we have not a high priest which cannot be **touched** with the feelings of **our infirmities;** but was in all points tempted like as we are, yet without sin.*

*Hebrews 4:15, NKJV: For we do not have a High Priest who cannot **sympathize** with our weaknesses, but was in all points tempted as we are, yet without sin.*

Jesus, our High Priest, can be **touched** with the feelings of "our infirmities" (lit., our weaknesses). Anyone who feels the Lord created him/her ugly (according to today's standards), remember, God made Jesus uglier (Isaiah 52:14b). Therefore, He can be "touched," or He can sympathize with our ugliness. The word "touched" is translated as "sympathetic." Thus, He is sympathetic towards all.

Jesus will let every individual know they are beautiful, even, compared to Him. He is able to aid (comfort) them that are tempted (Hebrews 2:18). Jesus was in **"all points** tempted as we are"** (Hebrews 4:15). This means, He was also tempted in the area of self-esteem. He was also tempted in the area of ugliness. So, smile, and feel good about yourself; the Lord is emphatic towards you. Jesus is our peace because **he embraces our**

ugliness. When I was living in North Carolina in the early 1990s, I was the teacher for a cell group of a local Church; and because this understanding of Jesus' ugliness was so real to me, I taught it immediately.

As I was relaying this word from God, a lady who was visiting the area began to weep. I stopped teaching, and asked her, "Why are you weeping?" She replied by stating that her son went to a particular church on a Sunday after being released from jail (her son at the time also had dreadlocks). The lady continued by saying that the Church cast her son out of the fellowship and called him "ugly" because he had dreadlocks, and because he was Black. As she continued to weep, she indicated how the word I was teaching blessed her. She also said she would tell her son about the good news of Jesus who accepted her son's ugliness.

As stated above, Jesus is our peace, **because He embraces our ugliness**; "the chastisement for our peace upon Him." Remember, Jesus is not a blond hair man, with blue eyes, as depicted in pictures invented by mem. Neither is he a handsome Black man with dreadlocks; and this image is also invented by men. Jesus is a Jew; and he may or may not have blue eyes; as some believe that the people of the tribe of Judah may have blue eyes.

He is the ugliest man God made. No one is able to draw a true representation of our Lord. First of all, **we were not there** when He walked the earth. Most importantly, the Scripture teaches that there is no representation of Jesus. **None can look like Him because He is one of a kind.**

What is Beauty?

There are many Hebrew words translated to mean beauty. One of them is **Yophiy (yof-ee).** The Hebrew pictograph **of "Yophiy" is that of what comes from-the activity of speech.** This may mean that beauty is also linked to speech.

The root word for Yophiy is **Yophah (yaw-faw), which** means **to be bright.** Therefore, **beauty is brightness,** and brightness has to do with "character" (compare Hebrews 1:3). Thus, beauty is **within;** or beauty comes from within. **Jesus said out of the heart the mouth speaks.!**

*Psalms 45:11, KJV: So, shall the **king** greatly desire thy **beauty (root: brightness)** for he is the Lord, and worship thou him.*

Psalms 45:13, KJV: The **king's** daughter is all glorious **within:** her clothing [within] is of wrought gold.

The "King" in verse eleven is the Lord. He greatly desires everyone's beauty (brightness). In other words, God wants to see His brightness in you as you "worship" him. In the words of Psalm 45:13, "The king's daughter is **all glorious within"** (Compare Songs of Solomon 2:14). His (God's) "daughter" (symbolic of the Church) is all glorious **within.** God sees true beauty as

40

brightness, **within.** This goes for all in the earth who have the brightness of God shining through their hearts (2 Peter 1:19). Therefore, regardless of what a person feels about his/her appearance, God considers that person beautiful when Brightness (Jesus') is on the inside (compare Matthew 6:22-23). **Therefore, ugliness is the opposite of brightness.** The opposite of brightness is darkness.

This darkness is on the inside of peoples' hearts, not outward appearance (2 Corinthians 4:6). There are many beautiful people outwardly; yet they are ugly on the inside. With this in mind, one can easily understand **"what"** makes one ugly.

The **"what"** is the ugliness of sin! This is why all of us must accept the Lord Jesus Christ, as Savior, Lord, and the Son of God. Sin, which causes ugliness, can only be healed by Jesus who can identify with humanity's ugliness to its fullest. The Church must be **timely** in presenting Jesus to this generation. Why? Beauty also has to do with **timing.** Remember, "He hath made everything beautiful in **his time...." (Ecclesiastes 3: 11, KJV).**

One of the Greek words translated to mean "beautiful" is **"horaious,"** which comes from the word **hora ("hour")** [see Romans 10:15]. **"Horaious"** means belonging to the right hour or season **(timely)** [Strong's # 5611]. This compliments the verse from the book of Ecclesiastes 3:11, partially stated above. Let us see how it is used in the book of Romans.

*Romans 10:15, NKJV: And how shall they preach unless they are sent? As it is written: "How **beautiful (lit., timely)** are the feet of those who preach the gospel of peace, who bring glad tidings of good things!"*

In this verse, we see beauty is preaching the Gospel (the good news). It is the beautiful (timely) message of the Gospel of Jesus that God sees as good. For example, the timely message of this book may be helping the reader, even now. How? The reader is hearing "glad tiding of good things!"

The **"good thing"** that Jesus can identify with one's ugliness is helping in the area of self-esteem. Thus, one becomes "glad" (happy) to hear such good news. Can you see it now? "He hath made everything **beautiful in his time"** (Ecclesiastes 3:11).

Yet, ironically, it is for this very beauty (brightness of the Gospel; 2 Corinthians 4:4) our Lord was killed. "Who being **the brightness** of His glory and the express image (lit., character) of His [God's] person ..." (Hebrews 1:3). Men despised His outward ugliness; and they also hated His light (the brightness of the beauty of Jesus' internal character). They hated His internal beauty because, to the persecutors, the Lamb's internal beauty did not match their expectation of God's behavior towards the sinners and depraved.

Jesus' beautiful news (the gospel of Jesus) that the poor can also have the King's domain working in their lives was not liked by the religious folks. Jesus' beautiful news that the tax collectors (the rich who collected taxes) can also be forgiven was not liked by the "orthodox" of His day.

Whenever the Lamb demonstrated beauty by comforting the depraved (poor depraved or the rich depraved) He was assassinated with words. This was apparently the treatment that was dished out to those who did not have the "beauty" according to the religious standard of that age.

Yet, in all the ugly appearances of the Lamb, He was able to comfort His followers out of His internal beauty. He knew He was from God, regardless of what He looked like on the outside. Jesus is from God; just as you and I are, no matter our appearances. It is the internal beauty that matters. He was made worthy to heal us, because of His love for His beautiful creation.

The **slain Lamb** is **worthy** to heal all who feel slain for their ugliness. The **ugly Lamb** can **comfort us** in all our pains. The Lamb of God restored positive self-concepts to His creation in spite of what our circumstances may look like on the outside.

He is our beauty in any appearance problem we may feel ashamed of. He is our comfort in any appearance problem we may face with our own faces. Jesus is the High Priest who comforts us in all our pressures of life that may appear contrary to the standards of this age. He overcame similar circumstances.

Ugly Circumstances, Priestly Comfort

For this chapter on ugly circumstances, priestly comfort, I will first cite scriptural references before I provide an understanding I received from our Lord Jesus. That is, there are many ugly circumstances listed in the Scriptures from which we can receive comfort.

*Hebrews 4:14, NKJV: For we do not have a High Priest who cannot **sympathize** with our **weaknesses**, but was in **all points tempted as we are**, yet without sin.*

*Matthew 8:19-21, N KJV: [19]Then a certain scribe came and said to Him, "Teacher, I will follow You wherever You go." [20]And Jesus said to him, "Foxes have holes and birds of the air have nests, **but the Son of Man has nowhere to lay His head."***

*1 Corinthians 4:9-11, NKJV: … **We have been made a spectacle to the world, both to angels and to men** … and **we are poorly clothed**, and beaten, and **homeless.***

*John 1:45-46, NKJV: [45]Philip found Nathanael and said to him, "We have found … Jesus **of Nazareth, the son of Joseph." [46]And Nathanael said to him, "Can anything good come out of Nazareth?"***

*2 Kings 2:23, NKJV: Then he [Elisha] went up from there to Bethel; and as he was going up the road, some youths came from the city and mocked him, and said to him, "**Go up, you baldhead! Go up, you baldhead!**"*

From the Scriptures above, we can see some of the ugly circumstances of life. You have Jesus who did not have a place to lay His Head. There is Paul (a sent apostle) and other Believers who were poorly clothed, homeless, and spectacles because of their circumstances. Jesus was raised in a bad city — Baltimore, Maryland, "oops," I mean Nazareth. Elisha was teased for his baldhead. This sounds like most of us, doesn't it? Those who are critical always see the outward "bad" and not the **inward good.**

You may have been brought up in an ugly city — the ghetto. This does not change the beauty that the Lord has placed **in** you. You can rise from that and move to a "heavenly city." You may be scantily clothed on the outside yet clothed with glory and honor "within." You may not currently have a certain dwelling place; yet there is a place in Jesus. Your hair may be falling out like Elisha. He (the Lord Jesus) can give you hair.

I remember in the early 1990's a Sister Believer came to me with her daughter's hair falling out; I mean, the young girl had nothing but patches of short hair. The situation for the young girl was "ugly." I laid my hand on her daughter's hair and prayed that her hair would be restored. The next time (about 30 days later) I saw the little girl whose hair had grown down to the middle of her back. Jesus comforted her by causing her hair to regrow. The Lamb can also comfort you; because He felt what all humanity feels deep on the inside. He gives beauty in place of ashes. He is our Sympathizer.

This is true for any other area of our lives. Jesus has been tempted in every way. Jesus was made a spectacle for our healing. This includes being judged for ugliness relative to beauty standards of the beast system. So, how does the Lord heals us? He heal us by pouring his love in us through the Holy Spirit (Romans 5:5, Ephesians 3:14-19).

He heals us by teaching us to love ourselves no matter what we or our circumstances look like. The Scripture teaches us to love our neighbor **as ourselves** (Luke 10:27). This type of love is the beginning. The greater love, or the "mature man" is to love others more than yourself as Jesus demonstrated (John 15:13).

With regards to loving your neighbor as yourself, a person can only treat (love) his/her neighbors the way he/she feels about his/herself. Another way of saying this is, the degree of "love" one has for himself/herself is the degree of love one can show to his/her neighbor. In other words, people treat other people the way they feel about themselves. So, people must love themselves, that is, accept how Jesus created them. Then, they can love their neighbors properly, even those neighbors who look down on people who do not look like them. This is accomplished as one realizes that Jesus was also tempted in this manner; yet He loved Himself and others.

Thus, Jesus can heal all who feel ugly according to this world's standard. Jesus knew that He was not ugly. He knew that he was "fearfully and wonderfully" made by God. He knew He possessed the beauty of God. Jesus knew Who He had on the inside — the Father of spirits, the Father of lights.

Remember the Lord loves you for who you are on the inside. **He forever stands as a High Priest to sympathize — having together-feeling — with us.** Now, I am not referring to our Lord having a pity party with our low thinking. What I am referring to is His confidence being discovered in us.

When one of the lame men that Jesus eventually healed was having a pity party concerning his circumstances, Jesus did not get commiserate with the man's ugly circumstance. He confidently asked the man, "Do you want to be made well?" Jesus then confidently said, "**Rise** ..." (John 5:1-9). I, therefore, pray that each of you, reading this, will allow the grace of our Lord Jesus to heal you completely. Let Jesus's esteem" "rise" in you. May you be confident in who you are on the inside through Him who is "within."   Believe in the Lord Jesus Christ; and your confidence (beauty) of the Lord within will eventually show on the outside.

OTHER BOOKS

Poiema, by Judith Peart
Wisdom from Above, by Judith Peart
Procreation, Understanding Sex, and Identity, by Judith Peart
100 Nevers, by Judith Peart
The Lamb, by Donald Peart
Jesus' Resurrection, Our Inheritance, by Donald Peart.
Sexuality, By Donald Peart
Forgiven 490 Times, by Donald Peart w/Judith Peart!
The Days of the Seventh Angel, By Donald Peart
The Torah (The Principle) of Giving, by Donald Peart
The Time Came, by Donald Peart
The Last Hour, the First Hour, the Forty-Second Generation, by Donald Peart
Vision Real, by Donald Peart
The False Prophet, Alias, Another Beast V1, by Donald Peart
"the beast," by Donald Peart
Son of Man Prophesy Against the false prophet, by Donald Peart
The Many False Prophets (The Dragon's Tail), by Donald Peart
The Work of Lawlessness Revealed, by Donald Peart
When the Lord Made the Tempter, by Donald Peart
Examining Doctrine, Volume 1, by Donald Peart
Exousia, Your God Given Authority, by Donald Peart
The Numbers of God, by Donald Peart
The Completions of the Ages, the Gate, the Door and the Veil, by Donald Peart
The Revelation of Jesus Christ, by Donald Peart
Jude—Translation and Commentary, by Donald Peart
Obtaining the Better Resurrection, by Donald Peart
Manifestations from Our Lord Jesus Christ as documented by Donald and Judith Peart
The New Testament, Dr. Donald Peart Exegesis
The Tree of Life, By Dr. Donald Peart
The Spirit and Power of John, the Baptist by Dr. Donald Peart
Is She Married to a Husband? by Donald Peart
The Ugliest Man God Made by Donald Peart

Does Answering the Call of God Impact Your Children? by Donald Peart

Victory Out-of-the Beast-the Harvest of the Earth by Donald Peart

Melchizedek by Donald Peart

Ezekiel-the House-the City-the Land (Interpreting the Patterns) by Donald Peart

Butter and Honey, Understanding How to Choose the Good and Refuse Evil by Donald Peart

Wholly Maturing, Wholly Inheriting, Spirit, Soul, and Body, by Donald Peart

Angels and the Supernatural by Donald Peart

CONTACT INFORMATION:

Crown of Glory Ministries
P.O. Box 1041 Randallstown, MD 21133
donaldpeart7@gmail.com

Made in the USA
Columbia, SC
23 February 2023